GOD's SONNETS

Copyright © 2011 by Sky Pharaoh

All rights reserved under International Copyright Conventions. Published in the United States by BroHawk Productions.

All of the poems in this collection are copyright © by Sky Pharaoh.

This book or any portion thereof may not be reproduced or used in any manner whatsoever without the express written permission of the publisher except for the use of brief quotations in a book review.

ISBN: 978-0-9987561-8-9

www.BroHawk.com

To my Lord and Savior Jesus Christ,

You have been the foundation of my life, the source of my inspiration, and the reason for my soul's existence. You have given me the gift of words, and I dedicate this book of poetry to you.

May the words that flow from my pen be a reflection of your truth, your love, and your grace. May they bring hope to the hopeless, comfort to the hurting, and encouragement to the discouraged. May they point the way to you, and draw people closer to your heart.

I pray that this book of poetry would be a testament to your mercy and righteousness, and that it would glorify your name. I offer it to you as an act of worship and obedience, and ask that you would use it to accomplish your purposes in this Universe.

Thank you, Lord, for your unending love and grace for inspiring and consecrating this manuscript of poems. May all the honor and glory be yours, now and forevermore.

Amen.

The Dead Sea Scrolls

In caves of Qumran, hidden from our sight,

Lay ancient secrets, waiting to be found,

Till chance revealed them to our modern light,

And mysteries of old, were then unbound.

The Dead Sea scrolls, a treasure of the past,

A glimpse into the minds of those before,

Their words and thoughts, forever meant to last,

A window into times we can't explore.

In Hebrew script, the scrolls reveal their tale,

Of prophets, laws, and wisdom to impart,

Their message timeless, though the ages pale,

Their relevance still echoes in the heart.

Oh, scrolls of Qumran! Thy voice we hear,

As history unfolds, and we draw near.

Bible

Oh, Bible, book of life, of truth, and light,
A balm of healing, for our wounded souls,
Your words, they bring us comfort, in our plight,
And guide us to the One who makes us whole.

In pages old, we find such rich relief,
From sorrow, pain, and doubt, and fear's embrace,
For in your wisdom, there is no belief,
That cannot find a path to saving grace.

With stories of the sick, the blind, the lame,
And how they found new life, through faith alone,
We see how in the Bible, there's no shame,
For all who seek the Lord, to make them known.

Oh, Bible, word of God, our hearts renew,
May we, through faith, find healing, born anew.

Old Testament

The Old Testament, a treasure trove of tales,

Of ancient times, and patriarchs of old,

Of prophets, kings, and judges, who prevailed,

And stories that have oftentimes been told.

From Genesis, where God's creation shone,

To Malachi, where prophecies foretold,

The coming of the Lord, to reign alone,

And lead His people, to a future bold.

In law and history, we find God's plan,

His covenant with Israel, so sure,

And though they strayed, He never left their hand,

But loved them, in their wandering, so pure.

Oh, Old Testament, a guide to life and love,

May we, like those before us, look above.

Book of Genesis

The book of Genesis, so full of grace,

Is where our story, as a race, begins,

God's mighty power, and His loving face,

Are shown in every page, as life begins.

In Adam and Eve, we see our fall,

And in the flood, the judgment of our sin,

But in the ark, God's grace is shown to all,

And Noah's faithfulness brings us back in.

Abraham, Isaac, Jacob, and their kin,

Are shown to us as models of belief,

Their faithfulness, though not without chagrin,

Is still an inspiration, pure and brief.

Oh, Genesis, the book of our creation,

May we be faithful, to our great salvation.

The History of Creation

In the beginning, God created light,

And separated darkness from the day,

He spoke and brought forth the celestial sight,

The universe in all its grand display.

He crafted skies, the sea, and land below,

Filled them with creatures, great and small in size,

Then, on the sixth, He made mankind to show

His love for all that lived beneath the skies.

And on the seventh day, God rested well,

Satisfied with all that He had made,

His power and glory all could tell,

For all the wonders of creation displayed.

God's love and power were evident to see,

In the first seven days of history.

When Adam met Eve

When Adam met fair Eve, a world was born

A love so pure, so new, so unexplored

A beauty that was never seen before

And hearts that beat as one, so long ignored

In garden fair, where flowers bloomed and shone

And all the creatures of the earth did play

The two of them did find a love unknown

And thus began the very first of days

For in that moment, when their eyes did meet

The world was changed forevermore, so bright

And from their love, the world was made complete

A love that burned so pure, so strong, so right

And though their time was brief in Eden's bower

Their love still blooms in every heart and flower.

When Satan Deceived Eve

In Eden's garden, Satan slithered sly

And whispered to fair Eve, a twisted lie

A serpent's tongue, so crafty and so wry

And with his words, he made her heart comply

He spoke of knowledge, power, and desire

And tempted her with thoughts so dark and dire

His voice a poison, meant to light a fire

Within her heart, and fan the flames so higher

And as she ate the fruit of knowledge's tree

She felt a rush of power, dark and free

But as the light of Eden's garden fled

She knew the price she paid, with tears she shed

For though the knowledge brought her a new sight

She lost the beauty of love's sweet delight.

Cain and Abel

In days of old, when man was new to earth,

Two brothers dwelt, with hearts so vastly split;

One meek and mild, of sacrificial worth,

The other, Cain, with jealous rage was lit.

Abel, the shepherd, offered lambs with care,

A pleasing gift unto the Lord above,

While Cain, the tiller, brought fruit to share,

But found no favor in the eyes of love.

With envy burning in his heart and mind,

Cain slew his brother, in a fit of rage,

And as he fled, his soul was left behind,

Forever marked with God's eternal wage.

Thus, the first family was torn apart,

And Cain was left to bear a guilty heart.

The Cheirograph of Adam
(Adam's contract with Satan)

In tales of old, a legend doth arise,

Of Adam's contract, signed with Satan's hand,

A pact that bore a most horrendous price,

And doomed all of mankind to mortal stand.

The Cheirograph, the contract's written form,

A binding pledge, in ink of blackest hue,

A promise made, to give up all that's warm,

And suffer for the deeds that they'd pursue.

Yet in this tale, a glimmer of hope shines,

As Christ, the Savior, offers a new way,

To break the curse, and free all of mankind,

From Satan's grip, and sin's dark, dismal sway.

Oh, Cheirograph! Thy legend's message clear,

To break the chains, and live in love sincere.

The Covenant of God

The covenant of God, a promise made,

A bond of love between the divine and man,

A pledge of grace that would not fade,

A covenant that none could ever ban.

From Abraham to Moses and beyond,

The covenant endured through trials and pain,

A steadfast light that always shone,

A hope that never waned, despite the strain.

In Christ, the covenant found its perfect form,

A sacrifice of love that none could match,

A covenant of mercy to transform,

A pledge of grace that would forever last.

Oh, covenant of God, a promise true,

May we abide in thee, forever anew.

Book of Enoch

In visions seen by Enoch, long ago,

A world beyond our own was brought to light,

With angelic hosts, both high and low,

And mysteries revealed beyond our sight.

The Book of Enoch, a scripture rare,

A journey through the realms of Heaven's lore,

With wisdom deep, and knowledge to ensnare,

Its words a gift, for seekers to explore.

Enoch, thy visions, a prophetic call,

To hear the voice of God, and see His plan,

To stand amid the angels, great and small,

And know the ways of both the Son and Man.

Oh, Book of Enoch! Thy truth we seek,

As we draw near, to mysteries of the meek.

Noah and the Nephilim

In ancient times, when man did multiply,

And wickedness spread like a noxious weed,

The Lord looked down with anger in His eye,

And vowed to cleanse the earth of evil's seed.

But Noah found favor in God's sight,

A righteous man who walked with Him in truth,

And thus he was tasked to build an ark in flight,

To save himself and all of earthly youth.

But there were those who were not of this world,

The Nephilim, whose origin unknown,

Their presence in the land did God's plan unfurl,

And made His wrath upon the earth be shown.

In Noah's time, the flood did thus ensue,

To cleanse the earth of sin and start anew.

The Noahic Covenant

In times of old, when floods did sweep the land,

And drown the earth in waters deep and wide,

A man named Noah, led by divine hand,

Built an ark to keep all creatures alive.

The rains did fall, and waters did increase,

And all was lost, save those within the ark,

Till finally, the storm began to cease,

And Noah saw a rainbow in the dark.

God made a covenant with man that day,

To never again flood the earth with rain,

And in the sky, the rainbow did convey,

A promise that the world would bloom again.

So let us remember the Noahic pact,

And cherish the earth, in love and respect.

Shem and Ham and Japheth

Shem, Ham, and Japheth, sons of Noah's ark,
Whose lineage flowed from ancient times afar,
Their stories told in scripture and remark,
A legacy that shines like guiding star.
Shem, blessed by God, the father of the Jews,
His descendants thriving in the holy land,
A line that saw the prophets and the muse,
And still today they walk upon the sand.
Ham, who saw his father's nakedness,
A curse that would befall his offspring's fate,
But still, he fathered mighty men of strength,
Who spread their reach across the ancient states.
Japheth, who fathered nations far and wide,
His people's reach extended to the sea,
Their legacy, a testament to pride,
A rich and varied tapestry to see.
Shem, Ham, and Japheth, sons of Noah's grace,
Their stories still alive, a timeless trace.

The Abrahamic Covenant

When Abraham was called to leave his land,

And journey to a place he did not know,

He trusted in the Lord's almighty hand,

And followed where His guiding voice did go.

The Lord did promise Abraham with grace,

A covenant that would forever stand,

To make of him a great and blessed race,

And multiply his offspring, great and grand.

Through Isaac, Jacob, and the tribes that came,

The promise of the covenant held true,

And in the Lord's almighty holy name,

Abraham's descendants multiplied anew.

So let us honor Abraham's great faith,

And keep the covenant in sacred grace.

House of Abraham

In ancient times, in lands so far away,

There stood a house that was renowned and blessed,

A place where Abraham did live and pray,

A home that welcomed all who were oppressed.

With open doors and hearts that shone with love,

This house became a beacon in the night,

A symbol of the faith that soared above,

And set the course for all that's just and right.

And though the ages passed, and empires fell,

This house remained, a testament to grace,

A place where pilgrims came to hear the tale,

Of Abraham and Sarah's noble race.

So let us honor this most hallowed space,

And keep the flame of faith within our hearts,

For in this house, we find a sacred place,

Where love and hope and peace will never part.

Abraham: Father of Three Faiths

Abraham, father of three faiths divine,

Whose faith and courage sparked a holy flame,

His life a testament to will and design,

A patriarch whose legacy remains.

From Ur he journeyed forth with wife in tow,

Called by his God to seek a promised land,

Through trials and tests, his faith would grow,

His heart and soul upheld by God's command.

To him, a son was born in old age,

The promised seed, the child of sacrifice,

And from his loins, a great nation would rage,

A legacy that echoes through all life.

Abraham, revered by Jew, Christian, and Muslim,

A beacon of faith whose light will never dim.

Jacob and Esau

In ancient times, two brothers came to be,
Born to a father of great wealth and fame,
Jacob, the younger, with a mind to scheme,
Esau, the elder, strong and wild and free.
Esau, a hunter, brought home savory game,
While Jacob, cunning, cooked up savory stew,
But when Esau, famished, his birthright threw,
Jacob, shrewdly, seized the prize in his name.
Then, when their father's blessing was to be,
Jacob, disguised, received it for his own,
While Esau, angered, sought revenge and glee,
With hate and rage and bitterness well-grown.
Thus, brothers once close, now forever torn,
A legacy of envy, hate, and scorn.

Israel and Palestine

A land once peaceful, now torn apart,
By hatred, fear, and endless strife,
As brother fights against his brother's heart,
And families mourn their loved ones' life.
The land of Abraham, Isaac, and Jacob,
Now a battleground for mortal foes,
As rockets fly and bombs ignite the sky,
And tears of sorrow, like rivers flow.
Oh, Israel and Palestine, how long will you fight?
How long will your children suffer in the night?
When will you lay down your swords and shields,
And learn to live together, in peace that yields?
May the God of Abraham, Isaac, and Jacob,
Shine his light upon you, and bring you back,
To the land of peace, where love can reign,
And brotherhood can heal all pain.

Twelve Tribes of Israel

Twelve tribes of Israel, a nation grand,

United in their faith and common goal,

A people chosen by the Almighty's hand,

To spread His love and teachings to the whole.

From Judah's line, the kings and rulers came,

And Benjamin, the smallest, held his own,

While Dan, the judge, did justice without shame,

And Gad, the warrior, fought with heart of stone.

With Zebulun, the seafarers sailed the seas,

And Issachar, the wise, did teach and learn,

While Naphtali, the graceful, danced with ease,

And Simeon, the fervent, did ever yearn.

And so, each tribe did play their part with pride,

And in their faith, they stood, and never died.

Exodus

The book of Exodus, a story grand,

Of Israel's deliverance, from slavery's hand,

With Moses, called by God's great command,

To lead His people, to the Promised Land.

Through plagues and wonders, they were set free,

With pillar of cloud and fire, God did lead,

Through parted waters, they crossed the sea,

And on Mount Sinai, His law, He decreed.

But in the wilderness, they did complain,

Their faith was weak, their hearts were prone to stray,

Yet God, in mercy, did not let them wane,

But guided them, by night and day.

Oh, Exodus, a story of God's grace,

May we, like Israel, trust in His embrace.

YHWH

YHWH, the name above all other names,

Majestic, holy, infinite in might,

The one who made the heavens and the flames,

Whose wisdom fills the earth with radiant light.

Unseen by mortal eyes, yet always near,

The God of Abraham, of Isaac, of Jacob,

Infinite love and grace, and not of fear,

Whose mercy reaches all, from shepherd to pharaoh.

YHWH, the great I AM, who spoke to Moses,

In fiery bush, revealing His design,

And led the people through the Red Sea's poses,

To freedom from their captor's cruel confines.

Oh YHWH, we bow before your holy throne,

And praise your name, forever and alone.

Moses and God on Mt. Sinai

Upon the mount, where earth did touch the sky,
The chosen one ascended with great care,
To speak with God, the one whom none deny,
The power and the glory he did bear.
And there upon that holy, hallowed ground,
The Lord did call to Moses, speaking clear,
In flames and smoke, a wonder to be found,
His voice like thunder, echoing in fear.
Yet Moses stood, unshaken by the sight,
And listened to the words that God did say,
The laws that would guide Israel's plight,
And lead them through their trials, day by day.
So on that mount, a man of faith did meet,
With God himself, and found his path complete.

Honoring the Ten Commandments

The Ten Commandments, law of God above,

A guide for life, a moral code of love,

A covenant with Him who reigns on high,

A call to live a just and righteous life.

To honor them, we must first understand,

The depth of meaning, purpose and demand,

To love the Lord with all our heart and soul,

And live our lives in ways that make us whole.

We must not worship idols, nor take His name in vain,

To honor Sabbath day, and keep it free from strain,

And honor parents, as they raised us with care.

We must not kill nor steal, nor spread deceit or lies,

Nor covet what is not ours, nor lust in others' eyes,

But seek to live in harmony, and love that's just and fair.

So let us keep these commandments as our guide,

And live our lives in ways that God prescribes.

The Mosaic Covenant

On Sinai's mount, the Lord did speak to Moses,
And gave him laws to guide the people's way,
A covenant that would forever hold us,
And lead us on to live in righteousness each day.

The Ten Commandments, written on stone,
Became a guide for all who would believe,
And through the ages, this covenant has shown,
That love and justice are the keys to receive.

With offerings, and rituals, and holy ways,
The Mosaic Covenant bound the people's heart,
And in obedience, they found the righteous praise,
Of God who would not let them stray apart.

So let us hold the Mosaic Covenant true,
And live in love, with faith and grace anew.

Leviticus

Oh Leviticus, book of holy law,

Inscribed with God's commandments for His folk,

Thou teacheth us the ways of righteous awe,

And guideth us to walk the narrow yoke.

In thee, we find the rules of sacrifice,

The offerings that cleanse and make us pure,

The rituals that lead to paradise,

The holy feast that brings us close to shore.

Thou showeth us the path of holy living,

And warneth us of sin's destructive ways,

Thou teacheth us the art of giving,

And guideth us to tread the righteous maze.

Oh, Leviticus, thou art a holy guide,

A lamp to light our paths and be our pride.

God's Embrace

In the embrace of God, I find my rest,

A place of comfort, where I am made whole,

Where all my fears and doubts are laid to rest,

And all my worries fade into the soul.

Within those arms, I find a love so true,

A love that knows no bounds, nor limit set,

A love that gives me strength to see things through,

And fills my heart with peace that lingers yet.

And though I wander through this world of strife,

I know that I am not alone, nor lost,

For in that embrace, I find new life,

And all my cares are paid, and all my costs.

So let us seek that loving embrace each day,

And live our lives in joy, and light, and play.

The Strength of Samson

In ancient times, a hero strong and true,
A man whose strength surpassed all mortal bounds,
A gift from God, to help his people through,
A power that in mighty deeds resounds.
Samson, a judge, whose strength none could deny,
A man who fought against the Philistine horde,
A power great, that made his enemies fly,
And gave his people hope, with shield and sword.
His feats were many, and his strength was known,
A lion he had slain with just his hands,
A thousand men he fought, and overthrown,
A power that few could hope to understand.
Oh, Samson! Thy strength a symbol true,
Of God's great power, and what He can do.

The Rise of Zion

From the depths of sorrow, Zion rose up,

A beacon of hope, a shining light,

In a world that had forgotten love,

And turned its back on what is right.

With faith as its shield and courage as its sword,

Zion marched forward, against all odds,

And in its wake, the world was awed,

By the strength and beauty of its cause.

No more the sound of weeping and despair,

But songs of joy and triumph filled the air,

As Zion rose up, with its people strong,

And proved to all, that love can conquer wrong.

So let us sing of Zion's glorious rise,

And pray that its light will never die.

Kind David

Oh, King David, you were a shepherd boy,

Whose heart was pure and full of love for God,

Yet fate had other plans, and you found joy

As ruler of Israel, with staff and rod.

Your harp did sing of praises to our Lord,

And slew Goliath with a stone so true,

Your reign was mighty, and your word adored,

As King and Prophet, wise and just to view.

Yet, even you, great David, did succumb

To passions dark, and fell from grace divine,

Your sin did bring much sorrow, and a glum

Reminder of man's nature, frail and fine.

But in the end, your legacy lives on,

As Psalmist, Warrior, and King, all in one.

The Davidic Covenant

When David was anointed as a king,

The Lord made him a covenant of grace,

To make his throne forevermore to ring,

And let his kingdom rise in righteous place.

Through wars and trials, David kept the faith,

And in his heart, he held the covenant true,

And when his son, Solomon, took his place,

The Lord's great promise shone anew.

With wisdom, wealth, and peace beyond compare,

The Davidic kingdom flourished bright and bold,

And though it faced the trials of time and care,

The promise of the covenant held its hold.

So let us honor David's heart and crown,

And hold the Davidic Covenant renown.

Solomonic Dynasty

From ancient Ethiopia, the kings did reign,

A dynasty of power, a legacy profound,

The Solomonic line, whose rule did sustain,

A people, a land, and a culture renowned.

Their kings, they claimed, descended from King David,

A holy lineage, divine in nature,

And so they ruled with righteousness engrained,

And justice as their guiding feature.

For centuries they held their throne secure,

Defying foreign powers, and war's turmoil,

And all the while, their culture did endure,

Their faith, their art, their music, and their soil.

The Solomonic dynasty, a legacy of old,

Their story, still told, in Ethiopia's fold.

When the Queen of Sheba met Solomon

Oh Queen of Sheba, fair and wise and true,

Who came to visit Solomon in pride,

And found in him a king of wisdom's hue,

Whose fame and glory echoed far and wide.

Their meeting sparked a love that could not fade,

And in their passion, a son was born,

A prince named Menelik, who was made

A king to rule, a leader to adorn.

From Solomon's seed, a new line arose,

And Menelik, a king of great renown,

Ruled Ethiopia with strength and prose,

And wisdom passed from father to son.

Oh Queen of Sheba, wise and fair and true,

Your legacy still lives, a tale anew.

Book of Ezra

The book of Ezra tells of God's great plan,

To bring His people back to their homeland.

After long years of exile in a foreign land,

God's mercy and grace extended His hand.

The people returned to Jerusalem,

To rebuild the temple of the Lord above.

They faced opposition from many a man,

But their faith and trust in God never waned or dove.

Ezra, a priest, led the people in prayer,

And helped them to renew their covenant with God.

He taught them to live in righteousness and care,

And to trust in God's love, even when times were hard.

This book reminds us of God's faithfulness,

And of the hope He gives in times of distress.

Book of Job

The book of Job, a tale of suffering,

Of trials, pain, and grief beyond compare,

A man of faith, whose troubles kept on bringing,

Yet still, he trusted God, with fervent prayer.

His friends, they came, with counsel and advice,

But in their words, there was no understanding,

For in their view, Job must have paid the price,

For hidden sins, he was not confessing.

Yet in the end, the Lord did answer Job,

With wisdom far beyond our mortal thought,

And Job, he saw, what he'd never known before,

The greatness of the God, in whom he sought.

Oh, book of Job, a lesson for us all,

To trust in God, though trials may appall.

Book of Psalms

The Psalms, a hymnal of the heart's lament,

A guide to prayer, a source of comfort true,

With every verse, the soul is surely sent,

To seek the Lord, and in His love renew.

In David's words, we hear a shepherd's call,

A heart of worship, deep and pure and true,

His praise to God, like incense, does enthrall,

And lifts our souls to heavenly vistas new.

But in the Psalms, we find more than just praise,

For in the depths of sorrow, we can see,

A voice that cries out, in so many ways,

For mercy, help, and grace, so rich and free.

Oh, book of Psalms, our guide in every hour,

May we find solace, in its holy power.

Psalm 23

The Lord is my shepherd, I shall not want,

In pastures green, He leads me by still streams,

With tender care, He heals my every haunt,

And in His love, my soul forever beams.

Though in the valley of the shadow dark,

I fear no evil, for He is with me,

His rod and staff, they comfort and embark,

My trust in Him, eternal and carefree.

He prepares a table, before my foes,

Anoints my head, with oil of gladness true,

My cup, it overflows, with grace that flows,

From His abundance, ever old and new.

Oh, Psalm 23, a hymn of love and peace,

May we find rest, in Your sweet and gentle release.

Proverbs

In Proverbs, wisdom's voice is surely heard,

A guide to life, a light upon the way,

The path of righteousness, it does afford,

And leads us to the source of life each day.

In Solomon's words, we find the treasure,

Of knowledge, understanding, and insight,

The teachings of the wise, beyond all measure,

To guide us on the journey, day and night.

For in the pages of this holy book,

We find the way to walk in righteousness,

To shun the crooked path, the lure and hook,

And find our joy, in God's pure holiness.

Oh, Proverbs, wisdom's voice, so clear and true,

May we embrace your teachings, all our days through.

Solomon the Wise

Solomon, the king of Israel's land,

A wise and just ruler, known to all,

With mind and heart, that few could understand,

He answered every question, great and small.

His wisdom spread, throughout the world, so far,

And kings and queens would seek his counsel true,

And marvel at his judgments, like a star,

That shone with truth and fairness, through and through.

But Solomon knew, that wisdom came from God,

And humbly sought His guidance, day by day,

And built a temple, where His people trod,

To worship Him, and in His love to stay.

Oh Solomon, the wisest of them all,

May we seek wisdom, and on God's grace call.

Ecclesiastes

Ecclesiastes, a book of wisdom old,
Penned by the Preacher, who saw life's distress.
He wrote of all the things that man may hold,
But found that they were vanity, no less.
He spoke of toil and labor, strife and pain,
And questioned what it all could truly mean.
He searched for purpose, but all was in vain,
Till he found joy in God, the unseen.
The Preacher taught that everything in life,
Is fleeting like a vapor in the air.
He urged us to enjoy each moment rife,
And trust in God, who gives us all His care.
This book reminds us of life's fleeting breath,
And points us to the One who conquers death.

Song of Solomon

The Song of Solomon, a love divine,

Penned by the wisest king of Israel.

He spoke of love, in all its sweetest shine,

And how it's worth more than the finest quell.

The lovers' words, in passionate embrace,

Exalt each other's beauty and their love.

Their hearts entwined, with gentle, tender grace,

A reflection of the Holy One above.

Their love, a picture of God's love for us,

A love that's pure and faithful to the end.

Their passion, kindled like the rising sun,

Is a gift from God, on whom we depend.

This book reminds us of love's sweet embrace,

And of the One who gives us endless grace.

Book of Isaiah

Isaiah, the prophet of great renown,

Spoke words of warning and words of hope.

He called for justice and a turning around,

And promised salvation for all who would cope.

He spoke of the coming of a chosen one,

A servant who would suffer for mankind.

He spoke of judgment for all that was done,

But also of mercy, for the broken to find.

Isaiah's words are filled with beauty and truth,

And point us to the God of all creation.

He spoke of a God who is faithful and true,

And of a coming kingdom of restoration.

This book reminds us of God's love and grace,

And of the One who gives us a holy place.

Babylon the Great has Fallen

Once proud and mighty Babylon, now fallen,
Its walls and towers crumble to the ground,
No more the sound of joy and revelry,
But only silence, broken by the sound
Of wind and sand, and ghosts of long ago,
That haunt its ruins, whispering of past,
When kings and queens ruled over all below,
And Babylon was great, and meant to last.
But time, that fickle mistress, had her way,
And brought down Babylon, with all her might,
And in her ruins, nature held her sway,
And covered all in shadows, dark as night.
Yet still, there is a beauty to be found,
In Babylon's demise, in nature's bound.

Oracle

Oh, oracle divine, of wisdom great,

Whose words hold secrets of the future's fate,

Through mystic visions, and prophetic sight,

You offer guidance in the darkest night.

With ancient wisdom, and celestial grace,

You pierce the veil of time, to show the way,

And in your words, we find a sacred space,

To seek the truth, and light the path each day.

Oh, oracle of old, with mystic lore,

Your words are whispered in the winds of time,

And though we may not know what lies in store,

Your wisdom guides us through the cosmic climb.

With gifts of insight, and prophetic voice,

You guide us on our journey of life's choice.

Book of Ezekiel

Oh, Ezekiel, a prophet's voice so strong,
A vision of God's glory, pure and bright,
With words of judgment, that could pierce the wrong,
And bring God's people, to repentance's light.

With imagery, so vivid and intense,
He painted pictures of God's holy wrath,
And yet, in mercy, there was still a sense,
Of hope, and restoration's righteous path.

His prophecies, they spoke of future days,
When Israel would be gathered, once again,
And in their land, they'd worship God always,
And know His love, that never will wane.

Oh, book of Ezekiel, a message clear,
May we, like him, the voice of God revere.

The Pen of God

The pen of God, a mighty tool of truth,
Inscribed with words that move the hearts of men,
Its ink a river flowing with the proof
Of divine wisdom, unrelenting yen.
Each stroke imbued with grace and majesty,
Its power felt in every turn of phrase,
A force that brings the soul to ecstasy
And leads us on to seek His holy ways.
With every letter, every mark it makes,
The pen of God reveals His perfect will,
A path to follow for our own sakes,
A guide to lead us higher, higher still.
Oh pen of God, how wondrous is thy might,
A shining beacon in a world of night.

New Testament

The New Testament, a story of great love,

Of Christ, the Son of God, who came to save,

A gift from heaven, sent down from above,

To offer grace, and rise up from the grave.

From humble birth, in Bethlehem's stall,

To the cross, where He took on all our sin,

His life was lived, to fulfill God's call,

To make a way, for all to come in.

Through teachings, parables, and miracles,

He showed us how to love, and how to live,

And in His death and resurrection, full,

He offers hope, and grace to all who give.

Oh, New Testament, a message bright and true,

May we, like Christ, live out the love He knew.

The Three Wise Men

In Bethlehem, where stars shone bright and clear,

Three wise men followed one that shone the most,

With gifts and faith, they journeyed far and near,

Guided by light, they reached the holy coast.

Each brought a treasure, gold, and myrrh and frankincense,

To honor Christ, the newborn King of Kings,

Their gifts were tokens of deep reverence,

For Him who came to earth with love and wings.

Their story still lives on, a tale of old,

Three seekers of truth, who followed the light,

With hearts full of faith, and wisdom untold,

They found the One who banished endless night.

So let us all be wise, like those three men,

And follow the light, to find our peace again.

Virgin Mary

Oh, Mary, mother of our Lord divine,

Chosen to bear the Savior of mankind,

You answered "Yes" to God's great design,

And by your faith, new hope for all we find.

In humble grace, you gave yourself to God,

And through your son, the world was soon redeemed,

For in His sacrifice, we're all now awed,

And by His love, our shattered lives are gleamed.

A virgin pure, and yet a mother too,

You showed us how to love, with open heart,

And in your life, we find a faith so true,

That from it, we can never more depart.

Oh, Mary, in your love, we see God's plan,

May we, like you, bring hope to all our fellow man.

Birth of a Savior

Oh wondrous news, a savior's born this day,

A precious gift, from heaven's hallowed halls,

The world rejoices, in a great display,

For this is what the prophets did foretell.

The shepherds hasten to the manger's side,

And wise men journey from a distant land,

To pay their homage to the newborn child,

And hold him gently in their loving hands.

His birth brings hope, to a world in despair,

A shining light, to guide us on our way,

A promise of redemption, pure and fair,

That will endure through every passing day.

Oh, blessed babe, so innocent and mild,

May we be worthy of thy love so wild.

Childhood of Jesus

Oh, wondrous child, whose birth did light the night,
A babe so pure, with halo 'round thy head,
In thee was housed the source of all delight,
As in a manger thou didst make thy bed.
Thou grew in grace and wisdom day by day,
In Nazareth, where all did know thy name,
Thou learned the crafts of carpenter and way,
And in thy heart, God's purpose didst proclaim.
In temple courts, thou didst confound the wise,
With questions that revealed thy great insight,
And Mary, pondering all these things, surmised
The destiny that lay before thee bright.
Oh, childhood Christ, thy path was set in love,
A life that led to all-encompassing dove.

Jesus in Egypt

In Egypt's land, where Pharaohs once did reign,

A holy family fled from Herod's wrath,

With Joseph guiding Mary and her babe,

They sought a refuge on a foreign path.

Through desert sands and bustling city streets,

They traveled far to find a place to stay,

And in a foreign land, they found retreat,

A place where they could rest and safely pray.

Young Jesus, in this land of ancient lore,

Was sheltered from the danger that pursued,

And in his tender years, he learned much more,

Of foreign tongues and cultures, thus imbued.

Though far from home, they found a blessed rest,

And in this time, they grew and were so blessed.

Description of Jesus

With eyes that shone like stars on winter's night,
And hair that flowed in waves of raven black,
A presence strong, with grace and love so bright,
He walked the earth, a beacon in his track.
His skin was olive, bronzed by sun and sand,
His hands were rough, from carpentry and toil,
Yet in his heart, a love so pure did stand,
A strength and kindness that the world did foil.
And though his form has been portrayed in art,
In countless ways, by many hands and hearts,
It's not his looks that make him stand apart,
But how he lived, with love as his great art.
Oh, may we see in every face we meet,
The love of Christ, so strong and ever-sweet.

Baptized by John the Baptist

Amid the desert's hot and arid land,

I came to John, the Baptist, wise and just,

And there, with heart and soul, did I demand,

The sacred rite of baptism and trust.

In waters deep, he plunged me 'neath the tide,

And as I rose, I felt a holy light,

A grace that filled me with a sense of pride,

And washed away my sins, both day and night.

For John had come, a herald of the Lord,

To bring a message of repentance true,

And I had heard, and heeded every word,

And so I stood there, pure and born anew.

And in that moment, as the sun did shine,

I felt the peace that only grace divine.

When Satan tempted Jesus

When Jesus fasted, Satan came to try,

To tempt Him with the pride of earthly gain,

And bid Him worship him, with all the lie,

That all the kingdoms of the world could reign.

But Jesus stood, and spoke with holy might,

And countered every sly, deceitful word,

"For it is written", He declared with light,

And thus the devil's schemes were seen absurd.

Oh Satan, who had tempted all before,

Could not deceive the Son of God, so pure,

Who knew that worldly wealth was but a lure,

And sought instead the will of God, secure.

So let us learn from Jesus' steadfast heart,

To trust in God alone, and never depart.

Jesus turns Water to Wine

When Jesus turned the water into wine,

A wedding feast was changed forevermore.

For in that moment, by His power divine,

The guests were blessed with something to adore.

The jars were filled with water to the brim,

But with a word, the liquid turned to red.

The host was stunned and asked, "Where did you begin?"

For he knew not the miracle Jesus had led.

The wine was tasted, and it was divine,

The finest vintage ever tasted by man.

The guests rejoiced and praised the Son of Divine,

For the miracle that was done by His hand.

This miracle showed Jesus' power and grace,

And how He blesses all who seek His face.

Jesus cleanse a man of Leprosy

When Jesus cleansed a man with leprosy,

A miracle was wrought that day indeed.

For all who saw it, their hearts were set free,

And faith in Christ began to take seed.

The man with leprosy, he cried out loud,

"Lord, if you will, you can make me clean."

And Jesus touched him, and the leprosy bowed,

And the man was healed, a sight to be seen.

In awe and wonder, people looked on

As the man was made whole before their eyes.

They marveled at the power of God's Son,

And praised Him with joyful, grateful cries.

This miracle showed that Jesus is true,

And His love and mercy are always new.

Jesus Performs a Miracle in Nain

In Nain, a city small, with hearts so low,

A widow mourned her son, so young and fair,

But in her grief, she did not yet know,

That Christ Himself, was soon to meet her there.

He saw her pain, and touched the funeral bier,

And in that moment, death itself did flee,

For Christ, the Son of God, had drawn so near,

And with a word, He set the captive free.

The widow wept with joy, and all around,

Were filled with wonder, and with grateful praise,

For in that act, a new hope soon was found,

And Christ's great power, was revealed in all His ways.

Oh, miracle of Nain, so wondrous, true,

May we, like Christ, in all our actions, pursue.

Jesus Heals Two Blind Men

Jesus, the Son of God, the Light of the world,
Encountered two blind men who longed to see.
Their hearts were filled with hope as they unfurled,
And cried out, "Son of David, have mercy on me!"
With love and compassion, Jesus drew near,
And touched their eyes, saying, "Let it be done."
Their sight was restored, and they shed a tear,
For the miracle of sight had finally begun.
These blind men now saw what they'd never seen,
The beauty of God's creation, all around.
They fell to their knees, full of praise and esteem,
For the grace and mercy, they had found.
This miracle showed Jesus' power and might,
And how He brings the blind into the light.

Twelve Apostles of Christ

Twelve men were chosen by the Son of Man,

To be apostles and to spread His word,

They followed Jesus, walked where He did stand,

And from His teachings, their faith was spurred.

Peter, Andrew, James, and John were first,

Called from their nets to leave all and follow,

Then Philip, Bartholomew, and Matthew,

James, the son of Alphaeus, and Thaddaeus too.

Judas Iscariot, the one who betrayed,

And Simon the Zealot, so fervent and strong,

Thomas, who doubted until he saw the way,

And Matthias, chosen to right the wrong.

These twelve men, from different walks of life,

Were called to spread the Gospel, end all strife.

Parable of the Mustard Seed

From tiny seed a mighty plant does grow,

A parable that Jesus did proclaim.

The mustard seed, so small and plain to show,

Can yield a tree that's great in size and fame.

Its branches reach up high into the sky,

A shelter for the birds to rest and sing.

From humble start, this plant can glorify,

And spread its blessings with a gentle wing.

So too, our faith can grow from small to great,

From simple seed to tree of noble worth.

With trust in God, our hearts can elevate,

And bear good fruit that brings abundant mirth.

May we hold fast to faith like mustard seed,

And in its growth, find grace to meet our need.

Jesus Feeds Five Thousand with Five Loaves and Two Fish

Upon a hill, a throng had gathered wide,

Five thousand hungry souls with empty plates,

With only loaves and fish, a meager tide,

But Christ would feed them all, and love create.

With thanks to heaven, he blessed the bread and fish,

And broke it up, with grace beyond compare,

And in his hands, a miracle of wish,

A feast for thousands, nourished by his care.

Oh, what a sight, to see the crowds so fed,

With leftovers enough for days to come,

A symbol of the love that Jesus shed,

And of the light that guides us ever on.

May we remember always what he gave,

And in his love and mercy, be saved.

Jesus Walks on Water

In Galilee, amidst the stormy night,

The waves were raging, and the wind did howl,

The disciples, filled with fearful fright,

Saw Christ approach, with steps so light and foul.

He walked upon the water, with such ease,

As if the sea were but a solid ground,

And with His voice, the winds and waves did cease,

And all was calm, as peace and love abound.

Oh, what a miracle, beyond belief,

To see the Son of God upon the waves,

To witness His divine and holy chief,

As He the storm and tumult did outbrave.

So let us trust in Jesus, evermore,

And follow Him, to reach that heavenly shore.

The Prodigal Son

The prodigal son, with wayward heart and mind,
Went far away, to seek his selfish gain.
He squandered all his wealth, with friends to find,
Till poverty and hunger caused him pain.
In deepest sorrow, he resolved to go,
And seek forgiveness from his father's hand.
He longed to be with those he used to know,
And leave behind his former, wasteful brand.
With open arms, the father welcomed him,
And threw a feast, to celebrate his son.
The prodigal was filled with joy within,
And felt his new life had just begun.
This parable shows how love and grace divine,
Can bring the wayward back to God's design.

He who is without sin shall cast the first stone

When Jesus spoke those words of wisdom true,

Amidst the angry crowd and stony glares,

A woman stood, ashamed and feeling blue,

Her sins exposed, her soul laid bare.

The Pharisees, self-righteous in their ways,

Sought to condemn her for her misdeeds,

But Jesus, in his infinite grace,

Saw beyond her faults and all her needs.

"He that is without sin," he boldly said,

"Let him first cast a stone at her feet."

And one by one, they dropped their stones and fled,

For none were blameless, none were truly neat.

Oh, how the words of Christ still ring so clear,

"Judge not, lest ye be judged," we ought to hear.

Thirty Pieces of Silver

Oh, thirty pieces of silver, once so prized,

The cost to betray with just a kiss of lips,

Judas' payment, his conscience compromised,

A deal made with the devil, for his trips.

He thought the sum was worth the risk he took,

To hand over his friend, to those in power,

But in the end, he was left with just a look,

Of sorrow and regret in his darkest hour.

The price he paid, was more than he could bear,

The guilt and shame, a burden on his soul,

A cautionary tale, for all to beware,

Of greed and treachery's inevitable toll.

Oh, thirty pieces of silver, a tale of woe,

May we learn from Judas, and choose a better road.

The Gospel of Judas Iscariot

In tales of old, a traitor's name is known,

As Judas' kiss, the sign of foul deceit,

Yet in a gospel, newly brought to throne,

His role is redefined, and truth to meet.

The Gospel of Judas, a document rare,

Reveals a story, veiled for centuries,

Of Christ and disciples, and their fates to bear,

And how a chosen one, fulfilled prophecies.

With words and deeds, the Savior's path is laid,

And Judas' part, a purpose to fulfill,

A trusted friend, with whom the truth was stayed,

And through betrayal, brought God's plan to still.

Oh, Judas! Thy name now held in new light,

As we discern, the role that led to might.

The Last Supper

Around the table, gathered one last time,

The Master and His followers, so dear,

To share a meal, and in His love to chime,

Before His death, that all too soon was near.

The bread, the wine, the symbols of His love,

And of His sacrifice, about to be,

The final act, that would His people move,

To see the love, and grace, that set them free.

But even as they ate and drank, so still,

A traitor sat among them, with a lie,

And yet, the Master loved him, with a will,

And gave His life, for him and all, to die.

Oh last supper, the momentous event,

That changed the world, and all that it had meant.

The Good Shepherd

The Good Shepherd tends his flock with care and love,

His watchful eye upon each tender lamb,

He leads them to the fields and streams above,

And shelters them with his strong, gentle hand.

He knows each one by name, their every need,

Their fears, their pains, their joys, he understands,

And with his staff and rod, he doth proceed,

To guide them to the pastures and the lands.

He risks his life to save the ones that stray,

And brings them back to safety and the fold,

He feeds them, nurtures them along the way,

And shields them from the dangers that unfold.

So let us follow in the Shepherd's way,

And trust in him to guide us through each day.

Pontius Pilate

The trial of Jesus by Pontius Pilate,

A moment in time that changed the course of history.

A man of innocence, yet accused of sedition,

His life weighed on Pilate's heart, a mystery.

The angry mob outside the governor's hall,

Demanded Jesus' blood, a sacrifice to their wrath.

Yet Pilate, knowing Jesus' innocence above all,

Sought to release Him, to walk a righteous path.

The words of truth, that Jesus spoke that day,

Resounded in Pilate's heart, to make him think.

His verdict wavering, as he wished to stay,

Yet the pressure mounted, to let Jesus sink.

Pilate's choice, a question for all mankind,

To stand for truth, or let the innocent be maligned.

Crown of Thorns

Upon his head did rest a crown of thorns,

A symbol of the pain he would endure.

A sacrifice of love that still adorns

The hearts of those who seek his love so pure.

Each thorn a sharp reminder of the weight

Of all the sins of man that he would bear,

And yet he chose to suffer for our sake,

His love and mercy for us all to share.

Oh, crown of thorns, a testament to love,

A sign of grace and sacrifice divine,

Reminding us of blessings from above,

And of the endless mercy that is thine.

May we remember always what you gave,

And in our hearts, your love forever save.

The Crucifixion of Christ

A crown of thorns upon his head, he stood,

A man of sorrows, in his final hour,

His love for us, unyielding, pure and good,

As he endured the pain, with love and power.

The nails, they pierced his hands and feet with force,

And yet he bore the agony with grace,

A sacrifice, of love, without remorse,

For all of us, to see our sins erased.

The mocking jeers, the soldiers' callous sneers,

Could not diminish his steadfast love,

For in that moment, he dispelled our fears,

And sent his spirit, to the heavens above.

Oh Christ, your love for us, beyond compare,

May we remember your sacrifice, and share.

INRI

Above the cross, inscribed in bold relief

A message etched in three languages bright,

The letters spelled a name beyond belief,

And shone like stars amidst the dark of night.

INRI, the words that told a tragic tale,

Of one who came to bear our sins and pain,

Who walked the path that none could ever scale,

And on the cross, his sacrifice did reign.

Yet in that name, we find a hope so true,

A promise of redemption and of love,

A light that shines through all we say and do,

Guiding us to heaven up above.

Oh, INRI, a symbol of our faith,

A reminder of the price he paid.

May we never forget the love he gave,

And in his grace and mercy, be saved.

The Resurrection of Christ

When dawn broke on that holy Easter day,

The world stood still, as if in deep repose,

The tomb where Christ was laid now empty lay,

And all creation marveled at the throes

Of death and sin that He had conquered there,

The chains of darkness shattered by His might,

And in that moment, all of heaven bare,

Rejoiced at the great triumph of the Light.

For He, who suffered, bled and died for all,

Had risen from the grave, alive and free,

And now our hope, our joy, our life, our all,

Is found in Christ, the Lord of victory.

So let us sing with joy, and let us raise

Our voices high in worship, love and praise.

Rising on the Third Day

On the third day, as dawn began to break,

The tomb where Jesus lay was opened wide,

The stone, once sealing it, was rolled away,

And all creation marveled at the sight.

For He, who suffered greatly for our sin,

Had promised He would rise again in power,

And now the victory was surely His,

And death itself had lost its hold forevermore.

The grave could not contain the Son of God,

Whose love had brought Him to this mortal earth,

And now He rose, triumphant and unmarred,

And gave us hope of resurrection's worth.

So let us stand in awe, and let us sing

Of Christ our risen Lord, our Savior King.

When Moshiach Arrives

When Moshiach arrives, the world will sing,
A new era dawning, a new beginning.
The darkness that held us will vanish in the light,
And hope will fill our hearts, dispelling the night.
The earth will rejoice, the trees will dance,
And all of creation will be given a chance
To thrive and flourish in perfect harmony,
As all of humanity lives in unity.
No more will we suffer, no more will we fear,
For Moshiach will bring an end to all tears.
Love and kindness will reign supreme,
As we bask in the glow of an eternal dream.
So let us prepare for that glorious day,
When Moshiach arrives, and forever we'll stay
In a world of peace, where love will abide,
And all of creation will stand side by side.

Spirituality

Oh, spirit divine! Thou art the source of light,

That guides our souls upon life's winding road,

And fills our hearts with love and pure delight,

And helps us bear the burdens of our load.

Thou art the wind that blows us where we may,

And leads us to the path that we must tread,

And in thy wisdom, doth show us the way,

To find the truth that lies within our head.

In meditation's realm, we find thy grace,

And feel thy presence in our hearts and mind,

And in that stillness, doth our souls embrace,

The love and light that thou art so inclined.

Oh, spirit divine! Thou art our guiding star,

That leads us to the path where angels are.

God's Grace

Oh God, your grace is like a gentle breeze,

That blows upon our souls and makes us whole,

A mercy that brings comfort and eases,

And gives us strength to face life's trials with control.

In times of trouble, when we feel alone,

Your grace surrounds us like a warm embrace,

A light that shines on us and makes us known,

And fills our hearts with hope and peace and grace.

For in your grace, we find a love divine,

A love that knows no bounds or limits set,

A love that reaches out to make us shine,

And holds us in its arms without regret.

So let us trust in your abounding grace,

And live our lives with joy upon our face.

The Gospel of Mary Magdalene

In ancient texts, a woman's voice is heard,

Whose name is known, for love beyond compare,

And though her story's often been obscured,

Her gospel speaks, of mysteries to share.

The Gospel of Mary, a testament true,

To Christ's teachings, and his message of love,

And in its pages, we find something new,

A woman's voice, that echoes from above.

With words of wisdom, and divine insight,

Mary Magdalene, reveals sacred truth,

And through her teachings, we find a path so bright,

A way to live, with love as living proof.

Oh, Mary! Thy gospel's voice we hear,

As we embrace, a love that's ever near.

John 3:16

Oh John, thy words doth bring such wondrous light

To hearts that seek salvation's holy grace

For in thy verse, there shines a love so bright

That all who read may see God's tender face

"For God so loved the world," thou didst declare

That He sent forth His only begotten Son

That whosoever would believe and dare

Shall have eternal life when life is done

Oh how this truth doth stir the soul within

And fills the heart with hope and boundless love

For in these words, we find the way to win

The gift of grace from heaven above

So let us cling to John's immortal line

And in its promise, may our hearts entwine.

The New Covenant

A new covenant, in blood of love and grace,
Was given to us through our Lord and King,
To cleanse our souls, and show us Heaven's face,
And let us rise on high, with angels' wings.

Through Christ's great sacrifice, we are made new,
And sin and death no longer hold their sway,
For in His blood, we find a life that's true,
And in His love, we find a brighter way.

The law is written on our hearts in love,
And through the Spirit's power, we are free,
To live in grace, and seek the things above,
And find our hope and joy in God's decree.

So let us hold the New Covenant with joy,
And in His grace, our hearts and souls deploy.

The Firstborn of the Dead

Oh firstborn from the dead, you rose with might
And broke the chains of death and sin apart
Your resurrection brought the world new light
And gave to us a hope that will not depart

You triumphed over death and every foe
And showed us all the power of your love
You gave us grace and mercy we don't know
And brought us life from heaven above

Now we, your children, can sing and shout
And praise your name forevermore
For you have conquered death without a doubt
And opened wide salvation's door

Oh firstborn from the dead, we praise your name
And worship you, our Savior and our King.

The Seven Churches

The Loveless Church, devoid of heartfelt love,
With empty rituals, void of compassion,
A place where God's grace seems to be unwove,
And love for one another is forgotten.
The Persecuted Church, oppressed and torn,
Enduring hardship, pain, and sacrifice,
A witness to the world, standing strong,
A beacon of hope that never dies.
The Compromising Church, swayed by the world,
Aiming to please, yet losing its own soul,
A place where truth and faith are often swirled,
And false prophets with their lies take control.
The Corrupt Church, consumed by greed and power,
Where leaders' hearts are cold and hard as stone,
Their motives impure, and morality sour,
Deceiving many with their lusts unknown.
The Dead Church, a shell of what it once was,
A place where life and spirit have since fled,
Where empty pews and apathy cause a buzz,
And hearts are hardened, and faith seems dead.
The Faithful Church, steadfast in its devotion,
Living out Christ's teachings day by day,
A place of worship, love, and strong emotion,
Where hope and joy and peace forever stay.
The Lukewarm Church, a mixture of both worlds,
Neither hot nor cold, and lacking zeal,
A place where compromise and comfort swirl,
And worldly ways cause passion to congeal.
May we remember those who came before,
And strive to be the faithful Church once more.

Lion of Judah

Oh Lion of Judah, we stand in awe of you,

A symbol of courage and regal might,

We pray that your reign shall forever ensue,

A testament to your power and your right.

The emblem of your tribe, forever true,

A lineage that stretches back in time,

Through trials and triumphs, you have come through,

And stand today, a symbol most divine.

The Lion of Judah, a symbol of hope,

To his people, a promise of salvation,

His courage, a guiding light to cope,

In times of strife, and in tribulation.

Oh, Lion of Judah, your name we revere,

A symbol of strength, a king without peer.

The Four Horsemen

Four horsemen, dark and fearsome in their might,
Ride forth across the land with dread intent,
Their galloping hooves a sound of blight,
As they bring forth war, famine, death, and pestilence.
The first, a conqueror with sword and shield,
He rides with fury and unbridled wrath,
His goal to conquer, to make foes yield,
And bring an end to peace in his warpath.
The second, famine, with his withered crop,
Leaves hunger in his wake, a cruel fate,
His victims left with nothing but to stop,
And suffer in despair, their hunger to sate.
The third, a rider clad in blackened shroud,
Carries death in his wake, his scythe in hand,
He brings an end to all, both meek and proud,
And leads them to their final resting land.
The fourth, pestilence, a bringer of disease,
A scourge upon the land, with no remorse,
He spreads his sickness with a sense of ease,
And leaves a wake of death without recourse.
Oh, four horsemen, harbingers of doom and woe,
May we find a way to stem your endless flow.

The Seven Seals

In Revelation's book, a tale is told,
Of Seven Seals that hold the fate of all,
A power so great, both new and old,
That only God himself could enthrall.
The first seal, a rider on a horse,
Conquering with a bow and a crown,
His victory brings a sense of remorse,
As the world falls under his dark frown.
The second seal, a rider on a red steed,
Bringing war and bloodshed to the land,
His sword, a symbol of destruction, indeed,
Leaves nothing but chaos in his command.
The third seal, a rider on a black horse,
Holding scales to weigh the food supply,
His famine spreads, a most cruel force,
Leaving hunger and despair as he rides by.
The fourth seal, a rider on a pale horse,
Bringing death and darkness to the earth,
IIis powcr, a force without remorse,
As he brings to an end, both death and birth.
The fifth seal, a cry of the martyrs heard,
Their souls taken, their voices raised,
Their sacrifice, an eternal word,
Their faith in God, forever praised.
The sixth seal, a great earthquake and wrath,
The sun and moon darkened, the stars fell,
The earth in chaos, as nature's path,
Revealed the power of God's mighty spell.
Oh Seven Seals, a testament of fate,
May we find the strength to stand, before it's too late.

Seven Archangels

Amidst the heavens, seven angels reign,
The archangels, with powers most divine,
Each blessed with gifts that they do maintain,
To guide and protect all of mankind.
First there's Michael, strong and bold of heart,
The leader of the heavenly host,
He wields his sword and tears evil apart,
Defending those who need it most.
Next comes Gabriel, God's messenger true,
Whose trumpet heralds joy and love,
He brings glad tidings to me and you,
From the heavens up above.
Then Raphael, the healer, takes his place,
With powers to mend both body and soul,
His grace and compassion soothe with grace,
Making the sick and broken whole.
Uriel brings the fire, the light of truth,
To banish lies and deceit's dark sway,
His sight can pierce through shadows and soothe,
Guiding us towards a brighter day.
Jophiel, with beauty that doth inspire,
Creates the wonders that we can see,
His art and grace light our inner fire,
Showing us the power of harmony.
Finally, Chamuel, angel of love,
Finds the lost and leads them to the way,
His tender heart lifts us up above,
To a world where hope and peace hold sway.
Thus, in the heavens above us all,
The archangels stand guard, and never fall.

Michael the Archangel

Oh, Michael, thou archangel, great and true,

A warrior of heaven, pure of heart,

Thy sword is sharp, thy shield forever new,

Thy courage never falters, from the start.

With wings of white, thou soarest through the sky,

And with thy strength, the devil's schemes are crushed,

Thy battle cry doth make the fallen fly,

And all thy foes, beneath thy might, are hushed.

Thou art the guardian of the holy realm,

A sentry to the gates of paradise,

Thy gaze is firm, thy vigil at the helm,

And thou art ever faithful, to thy prize.

Oh, Michael, patron saint of warriors bold,

Protect us, as we tread the paths of old.

Mark of the Beast

Amidst the chaos of a world undone,

There lies a symbol, feared by all who know

The tales of dark, and evil deeds undone

That speak of power, from the depths below.

The mark of the beast, a cursed tattoo,

That brands the flesh of those who dare defy

The tyrant's rule, and all that he construes

To be his law, and all that he decries.

But those who bear this mark, they know full well

The price they pay, for power and control

Is steep indeed, a living hell

That few can bear, with mind and soul whole.

So heed this warning, and do not be swayed

By promises of power, so easily made.

King of Kings and Lord of Lords

The King of Kings and Lord of Lords, divine,
His throne above all thrones, his rule supreme,
The one who reigns o'er all the earth and time,
The one in whom all things are made to gleam.

His power knows no end, his love so pure,
His wisdom far beyond our human thought,
His mercy, grace, and goodness all endure,
His justice righteous, always fairly wrought.

In majesty he sits, the Sovereign One,
His glory shining bright for all to see,
The Father's beloved, the only Son,
Who gave himself to set all captives free.

Oh, let us bow before the King of Kings,
And with our praises, let his throne resound,
For he alone is worthy of all things,
The one who saves and in his grace abounds.

Serpent of Old: Bound 1,000 Years

In ancient times, the serpent did deceive

With silver tongue and twisted mind so sly

He tempted Eve, and thus did cause to leave

Her perfect state, and innocence, goodbye

But justice came, and punishment was dealt

The serpent was condemned to be bound fast

For one thousand years, he would not be felt

His power broken, his dark days now past

Yet still he waits, with venom in his heart

For his release, when he shall strike again

And tear apart the world, and tear apart

The hearts of men, who'll fall to sin and pain

But let us not forget the thousand years

And bind the serpent once again, with tears.

The Alpha and the Omega

Jesus, the Alpha and Omega, grand,

The first and last, beginning and the end,

He who created all, with outstretched hand,

The one who calls us friend, and on him depend.

Before the dawn of time, he was with God,

The Word made flesh, in whom all things were made,

The light of life, who suffered 'neath the rod,

And on the cross, for our sins, he paid.

He is the bright and morning star, who reigns,

The one who conquers death, and gives us life,

In him, we find our hope, our joy, our gains,

And in his grace, we're free from sin and strife.

So let us sing of him, the First and Last,

The King of Kings, who loves us unsurpassed.

The Bright and Morning Star

The Offspring of David, bright and true,
The promised One, foretold in ancient days,
The one who came to make all things anew,
And shine a light upon the world's dark ways.

A star that rises in the morning sky,
And leads us on to paths of hope and grace,
A guide that never fails, though troubles nigh,
And gives us strength to run the faithful race.

The son of Jesse, born in Bethlehem,
Yet raised up high to reign on David's throne,
His kingdom, one that never will condemn,
His love and mercy, ever brightly shone.

So let us lift our voices to the skies,
And sing of him, the Bright and Morning Star,
For he alone can make our hearts arise,
And lead us on to all that's good and fair.

"Surely I am coming quickly"

"Surely I am coming quickly," he said,
The promise of the Lord, the King of Kings,
The one who suffered in our stead,
And conquered death to bring us greater things.
The hope that we have, the joy we find,
Is all because he kept his promise true,
The one who heals the broken heart and mind,
And gives us strength to see the journey through.
He's coming soon, though we may not know when,
To take us home, to be with him above,
To rest forevermore, free from sin,
And dwell in endless grace and perfect love.
So let us live our lives with him in view,
And keep the faith until his promise's due.

God's Word

Oh word of God, a balm to wounded hearts,

A light to guide the path of life's long way,

A promise given that will ne'er depart,

A hope that strengthens for the coming day.

In ancient times, your truth was often heard,

Inscribed on tablets and on scrolls of old,

And though the world may change with every word,

Your message still rings out, steadfast and bold.

From Genesis to Revelation's end,

Your wisdom speaks to all who lend an ear,

And in our hearts and souls, we comprehend

Your message, which we hold so ever dear.

So let us take your word and make it known,

And in its truth and light, our lives be shown.

The Rapture

In the twinkling of an eye, it shall come,

The rapture, when the faithful shall ascend,

To meet the Lord, in his eternal home,

A joyous reunion, without an end.

The trumpets shall sound, the skies shall open wide,

And those who have believed, shall be caught up,

Their souls, in a moment, glorified,

Their hearts, overflowing with love's sweet cup.

The dead in Christ, shall rise first, to meet the Lord,

Then those who remain, shall be caught away,

Their mortal bodies, now forever restored,

To stand before the throne, on that eternal day.

Oh rapture, a promise of hope and grace,

May we be ready, when you come to take our place.

Heaven

Oh, Heaven! Thou art a realm beyond compare,

A place of beauty, love, and pure delight,

Where angels sing and joy is everywhere,

And in thy presence, all is pure and right.

Thou art the home of all the blessed souls,

Who've left this world to rest in thy embrace,

And in thy grace, their spirits find new roles,

In blissful peace and everlasting grace.

Thou art a vision of a world divine,

Where love and harmony forever reign,

And in thy light, we glimpse a sacred sign,

Of hope and joy that ease all mortal pain.

Oh, Heaven! Thou art a realm of purest light,

A place of wonder where all souls unite.

www.ingramcontent.com/pod-product-compliance
Lightning Source LLC
Chambersburg PA
CBHW060400050426
42449CB00009B/1821